WILLIAM BLAKE

INTRODUCTION BY
Mark Crosby

BODLEIAN
LIBRARY
PUBLISHING

Mark Crosby is an associate professor of English at Kansas State University and a fellow of the Society of Antiquaries.

First published in 2024 by Bodleian Library Publishing
Broad Street, Oxford OX1 3BG
www.bodleianshop.co.uk

ISBN: 978 1 85124 642 7

Introduction and transcriptions © Mark Crosby 2024

Images from Oxford, Bodleian Library, Arch. G e.42 © Bodleian Libraries,
University of Oxford, 2024
This edition © Bodleian Library Publishing, University of Oxford, 2024

Publisher: Samuel Fanous
Managing Editor: Susie Foster
Editor: Janet Phillips
Picture Editor: Leanda Shrimpton
Designed and typeset by by Dot Little at the Bodleian Library in 11/14pt Monotype Fournier
Printed and bound in China by C&C Offset Printing Co., Ltd on 140 gsm Chinese Golden Sun paper

British Library Catalogue in Publishing Data
A CIP record of this publication is available from the British Library

CONTENTS

William Blake's *Songs of Innocence*

'Innocence dwells with Wisdom but never with Ignorance'
WILLIAM BLAKE

Born on 28 November 1757, William Blake grew up in London
and from a young age displayed a precocious talent for drawing.
Encouraged by his father, a hosier by trade, the ten-year-old Blake
enrolled at Henry Pars's drawing school on the Strand. Under Pars's
direction, Blake learned to sketch the human form by copying casts
of classical statues. He also began collecting prints by Albrecht
Dürer and after paintings by Raphael and Michelangelo. When Blake
entered the professional world, he initially wanted to apprentice at a
painter's atelier, but this proved too costly. A less expensive option
came through Pars's connections with the less prestigious profession
of engraving and, at the age of fourteen, Blake was apprenticed to
the master engraver James Basire.

Blake spent seven years living and working with Basire. One
of the finest line engravers in Europe, Basire spent time in Rome
sketching designs after Raphael and Michelangelo. When Blake
became his apprentice, Basire was the official engraver to the Royal
Society and the Society of Antiquaries. Under his master's tutelage
Blake learned etching and engraving techniques known as intaglio
graphics. Basire's robust linear style was markedly different from

SONGS
OF
Innocence

The Author & Printer W Blake

many of his contemporaries and was an extremely time consuming method that took patience and skill to master. Blake proved a quick learner on the evidence of his earliest engraving (1773) after a figure in Michelangelo's *The Crucifixion of Saint Peter* (1549), later retitled *Joseph of Arimathea among the Rocks of Albion*. Basire also clearly considered Blake an accomplished draughtsman because in 1773 he sent his apprentice to Westminster Abbey and Temple Church to make a series of sketches of the Royal tombs and other Gothic monuments.

At the end of his apprenticeship in 1779, Blake entertained hopes of establishing himself as an artist and was admitted as a student at the Royal Academy, taking drawing classes and exhibiting work at the Academy's annual exhibitions. One of the leading painters of era, George Romney, remarked that Blake's early drawings were comparable with Michelangelo. Blake also set up a short-lived print shop with another of Basire's former apprentices and embarked on a career as a commercial engraver, mainly producing prints after other artists to illustrate books.

The years following his apprenticeship were busy. On 18 August 1782 Blake married Catherine Boucher, the daughter of a market gardener. He also attended a literary salon hosted by the Reverend A.S. Mathew and his wife, Harriet. At these gatherings Blake read and, according to another member of the salon, sang poems to tunes that he'd been composing since childhood. With the help of the Mathews and their circle, these juvenile poems were privately published as *Poetical Sketches by W.B.* in 1784. Around the same time, there was an unsuccessful attempt to send Blake to Italy to study classical sculptures and the Renaissance masters. He also composed an absurdist drama, now known as *An Island in the Moon*, that was inspired by his experiences at the Mathews salon. This riotous satire takes place in various domestic settings located on the moon and is populated by an array of characters with names such as Inflammable Gass the wind finder and Sipsop the Pythagorean. These characters share gossip, tell rude jokes, and argue, often passionately, about contemporary issues. Characters also sing. Towards the end of the drama, Obtuse Angle performs a song called 'Holy Thursday', followed by Mrs Nannicantipot who sings 'Nurse's Song', and Quid the Cynic, who may be Blake's own self-parody, serenades his companions with 'The Little Boy Lost'. Blake includes versions of all three poems in *Songs of Innocence*.

Another character in *An Island in the Moon*, Suction the Epicurean, may be based on Blake's younger brother, Robert. The brothers were extremely close. Blake encouraged Robert to draw and nursed him during a terminal illness. When Robert died in 1787, Blake was devastated but for the remainder of his life considered Robert a wellspring of inspiration. By 1788, Blake was experimenting with engraving techniques as he sought to publish his own work and recalls that Robert came to him in a vision, revealing a method of relief etching that combines text and design on the surface of a copperplate. Relief etching enabled Blake to compose directly on the copper, painting images with a brush and writing text with a pen much like an artist painting on paper or canvas or an author writing a manuscript. Blake called this method illuminated printing and described it was a way to combine 'the Painter and the Poet'.

Blake's illuminated printing differs from the *intaglio* techniques that he'd learnt as an apprentice and used as a commercial copy engraver. *Intaglio* graphics were the primary way eighteenth-century engravers reproduced original images in prints, and involves making small incisions in the surface of a copperplate. This was achieved in two ways: using a tool called a burin to make lines or dots directly into the copperplate, or using acid to etch away areas of the surface. To etch a copperplate, the surface was covered in an acid-resistant varnish and then smoked using soot from a candle to create a black surface. An etching needle reproduces the original design by scratching lines into the sooted surface to expose the copper. A small wax dam was built around the edges of the plate and acid poured on to the surface, corroding the exposed metal. Once the etching was complete, the varnish was removed and ink applied using dabbers or inking balls to force the ink into the incisions. In both techniques, the engraver reverses the right-left orientation of the design being copied to replicate the orientation of the original when printed. A rolling press printed the plate, with the rollers exerting sufficent pressure to force the ink out of the incisions and onto a sheet of damp paper. Like his engraving master Blake used the mixed method, combining an initial etching stage followed by engraving for his commerical work.

For illuminated printing, Blake adapted the etching technique. Rather than cover the whole copperplate with varnish, Blake used a fine horse hair brush dipped in warm varnish to draw on the surface of the plate. For the text, he used a quill pen or stylus loaded with diluted varnish. When the varnish touched the metal, it cooled. As with *intaglio*, the left-right orientation is reversed when printed, which meant that Blake drew his designs and wrote his text backwards. As a trained engraver, Blake was skilled in rendering images in reverse and the more illuminated books he created, the more proficient he became in mirror writing. Blake would sometimes use an etching needle to scratch lines into areas that he had varnished before building a wax dam around the edges of the copperplate and applying acid. Once etched, the designs and text stood in relief and the plate would be cleaned. Ink was applied to the relief areas and Blake and his wife passed the plate through the rollers of their own starwheel rolling press. The areas incised in the varnish appear white against the inked background and is a technique, known as white-line etching, that Blake used to add definition and form to images.

Blake's relief-etching method was autographic, enabling him to compose directly on to the surface of the copperplate without the need for a preliminary drawing or draft text. And while there are examples of drawings and poems in manuscript that have been relief etched, illuminated printing afforded Blake the creative freedom to modify, revise, and invent as he composed on the plate. We see evidence of the auographic approach in 'The Chimney Sweeper', where in line 15 Blake began to write 'run', got as far a 'r' and ran out of space. He left the 'r' in place and above wrote the word in full. Similarly, in 'HOLY THURSDAY' Blake ran out of room at the end of the third line, writing 'snow' above the final word 'as'. Illuminated printing also encouraged variation and experimentation as the Blakes used different printing inks and watercolour washes for colouring on individual print runs. This method also unifies the division of labour inherent in eighteenth-century publishing. Instead of involving various professions to produce an illustrated book, illuminated printing gave Blake complete control over the entire process: he was the author, designer, illustrator, etcher, printer and colourist (with his wife), and publisher.

In 1789 Blake used illuminated printing to create an anthology of lyric poems illustrated with mostly bucolic designs called *Songs of Innocence*. It appears that for the initial print run, the Blakes made between seventeen and eighteen versions of *Songs of Innocence*. There are currently twenty-five extant versions of *Songs of Innocence* and from 1794, Blake began to combine *Innocence* with another group of lyric poems to create *Songs of Innocence and of Experience Shewing the Two Contrary States of the Human Soul*. The version of *Songs of Innocence* reproduced in this edition is known as copy L and was bequeathed to the Bodleian Library in July 1940 by Miss A.G.E. Carthew, who acquired it before 1921 (possibly from the dealer E. Pearson and Sons, who bought it at Sotheby's on 22 July 1902 for £19.10s). The early history of the Bodleian's *Songs of Innocence* is not known, but internal evidence dates it to the first print run of 1789. It was printed by Catherine in raw sienna ink and coloured, possibly by both William and Catherine, in translucent watercolour washes with some pen and ink work. Copy L comprises twenty-seven plates printed recto/verso, including two poems, 'The School Boy' and 'The Voice of the Ancient Bard' that Blake moved to *Songs of Experience* after 1794. The Bodleian's *Songs of Innocence*, however, lacks three poems often found in other versions: 'A Dream', 'The

Little Girl Lost', and 'The Little Girl Found'. There are three stitch holes on each page possibly made by William or Catherine to bind the poems together, although the current order of the poems may owe more to the binder of the pages in the early twentieth century than to the Blakes.

Blake mirror wrote all the poems in upright Roman miniscule with the exception of 'The Voice of the Ancient Bard' which is in pseudo-italic letters. Once printed, Blake enhanced many titles with pen and ink and other parts of the text on a few plates. In some instances, such as 'Infant Joy', Blake enhances words and letters with pen and ink. With 'Spring', he used watercolour to overwrite letters. The correspondence between the blue and red watercolour overwriting and the watercolour washes on the designs of 'Spring' suggest that colouring and enhancing the text were part of the same continuous and coordinated process. On one occasion, this hand colouring obscures the word 'tear' at the end of line 31 of 'On Anothers Sorrow'. By contemporary standards, Blake's spelling and punctuation can, at times, seem erratic. For example, he reverses the e and i in receive and adds an extra 'c' to echoing. His commas and full stops, which can be affected by the printing process and subsequent colouring, are challenging to decipher and the accompanying transcriptions preserve what can be read in the Bodleian's *Songs of Innocence*.

The poems of *Songs of Innocence* seem deceptively simple. Blake uses monosyllabic words and repetition with strong rhyme schemes and irregular accent patterns and line lengths. In Blake's regional accent certain slant rhymes like 'name' and 'lamb' may have been closer to true rhymes. While the versification is typical of the hymnal tradition and nursery rhymes, Blake composed his lyric poems with care and skill to present the realm of innocence as a space of play, harmony, and spontaneity, and where values like compassion and empathy are valued. At times irony may be detected with Blake gesturing to pressing social issues of his time, such as the exploitation of orphans and their horrific fate in 'The Chimney Sweeper'. A key theme of the collection is the immanence of Christ, who offers a mediating presence between God and humanity and is invoked both verbally and visually in figures such as the shepherd, the lamb, and the child.

Christ as a shepherd is depicted in the tailpiece of 'The Little Black Boy', a poem that from our contemporary perspective may be considered troubling. The speaker of the poem is the titular little black boy whose imagined interactions with an English (white) child highlight racial difference and gesture to eighteenth-century European notions of white superiority. There are no direct references to slavery, although the allusion to Africa as 'the southern wild' and the speaker's subordinate position indicates the internalization of the European values underpinning the slave trade. Blake was aware of, and influenced by, the abolitionist movement, and the same year that *Innocence* was self-published, William Wilberforce delivered his famous parliamentary speech calling for the abolition of slavery. Blake's poem tackles slavery and abolition through the boy's recollection of his mother's story, which reverses European attitudes to Africa by presenting blackness as a sign of divine love. In the final two stanzas, the speaker imagines transcending racial difference in heaven. Yet this apparent post-racial conclusion isn't quite what it seems as the boy still occupies a subordinate position, hoping to be loved by the white child once they become disembodied souls. The accompanying image shows the physical bodies of the children with the white boy closest to Christ, hands in supplication in a pose evoking Josiah Wedgwood's famous abolition emblem 'Am I not a Man and a Brother' from 1787, with the 'Little Black Boy' standing behind. While the poem begins by telling us that we're all alike in God's love, by the end we may detect irony with Blake exposing the limitations of an abolition movement informed by Christian values. Such values not only envision emancipation occurring in the afterlife, but also that the emancipated souls ought to be grateful for their posthumous freedom.

Many of the designs accompanying the poems depict pastoral spaces, such as village greens and woodland, populated with children, parental figures, and flocks of sheep. Other designs, such as the head and tail vignettes for 'HOLY THURSDAY', show clusters of children from London charity schools. The design for 'A Cradle Song' is the only indoor setting, depicting a mother or nursemaid leaning over an infant in a crib. Occupying over half of the page, this design evokes Renaissance depictions of the Virgin and child such as Raphael's masterpiece *Madonna di Loreto* (c.1511), copies and engravings of which circulated during Blake's time. The other head and tailpiece designs are indebted to eighteenth-century decorative book illustration. As a professional copy engraver Blake became immersed in this tradition during the 1780s, engraving illustrations for books after his friend, the artist Thomas Stothard.

Particular designs in *Songs of Innocence*, such as 'Laughing Song' and 'The Ecchoing Green', derive from Stothard's compositions. Unlike Stothard, Blake attends to the musculature of figures, which are reminiscent of the Renassisance masters, and also provides decorative borders using flowing lines to render vegetation with long tendrils that occasionally intrude on the text.

Trees are also a recurrent motif forming the borders for some designs and protective spaces for figures to sit or play beneath. Tiny human figures recline amongst branches, vines, and lettering, and interlinear motifs are scattered among the poetry. Blake's use of vine imagery and its association with Christian iconography echoes the content of many of the poems, and invokes the long tradition of devotional illustration found in medieval illuminated manuscripts. While Blake may have had only a brief encounter with such manuscripts during his time in Westminster Abbey, he was familiar with the decorative flourishes of vines and flowers on the Gothic tombs he sketched as an apprentice. Such border imagery in *Songs of Innocence* is more than decorative, with the vine symbolizing Christ's presence and the tiny humans and animals inviting allegorical readings in the tradition of biblical exegesis, with some of these figures representing the soul ascending from the material world to redemption. In other cases, the marginal motifs comment on, or amplify themes of, the poems. The minute human figures trapped in vines in 'A Cradle Song' may hint at a possible future for the swaddled infant. The vignettes occupying the tendril bowers bordering the 'Introduction' poem may function as a visual contents list, showing a series of outdoor scenes that anticipate the pastoral setting of many of the poems. These designs complement the poem, which offers an ontological explanation for the collection.

William and Catherine used a palette of primary colours, with blue, red and yellow translucent washes recurring throughout *Songs*. The Blakes combine strong reds and yellows in the sunrise and sunset designs that contrast with greens of the vegetation and blues of skies or the body hugging clothing associated with dancers in the eighteenth century. In 'The Little Boy Lost' and 'The Little Boy Found' designs, the palette is restricted to dark grey/brown with occasional strokes of yellow, red, and blue that accentuate the white clothing of the boy and God the father. Unlike later copies of *Innocence*, the colouring in the Bodleian version is at times effervescent, delicate, and subtle, perhaps even tentative as the Blakes developed their colour scheme.

Blake draws on the classical tradition with the pastoral settings of the poems and designs evoking Virgil's *Eclogues*, but his biggest influence was the eighteenth-century invention of childhood. By the time Blake created *Songs of Innocence*, the Rennaissance understanding of children as small adults requiring strict discipline had changed. Instead childhood was considered a time of vulnerabilty and development distinct from adulthood. Books of children's hymns, such as John Bunyan's *A Book for Boys and Girls* (1686) and Isaac Watts's *Divine Songs [...] for the use of children* (1715), are predicated on this view of childhood and were frequently reprinted during the eighteenth century. Bunyan offers the biblical pastoral of St. John's Christ as the good shepherd protecting his flock and, anticipating Blake's *Innocence*, Watts combines verse in the metre of English hymns with engraved images. Blake was also likely familiar with Charles Wesley's popular and much-reprinted *Hymns for Children* (1763) and Anna Barbauld's *Hymns in Prose for Children* (1781), which was published by Blake's main commercial employer during the 1780s, Joseph Johnson. The year before publishing *Innocence*, Blake illustrated Mary Wollstonecraft's *Original Stories from Real Life* (1788), also published by Johnson, with engravings after his own designs. By the time Blake relief-etched *Songs of Innocence*, he had ample evidence of a thriving market for a poetry collection imbued with Christian sentiments and directed at children.

Unlike these other eighteenth-century children's books, *Songs of Innocence* rejects strident moralism in favour of celebrating childhood as a state of unselfconsciousness that may be returned to at any age. For children, *Songs of Innocence* represents a familiar view of the world and hints at what will be lost in the transition to adulthood. For adults, Blake's remarkable collection asks us to view the world from a child's perspective, revealing the constraints of adulthood and offering the sort of insight and wisdom that comes with a less constrained, self-conscious perspective. Unfortunately for Blake, only friends and patrons were interested in such a book during his lifetime.

Since his recuperation by the pre-Raphaelite brotherhood and others, including the great Irish poet W.B. Yeats, Blake has become an enduring cultural presence with ubiquitous appeal. For some he's a mystic, a visionary prophet railing at institutional repression; for others he's a radical artist, an experimenter and iconoclast striving against the eddies and currents of history. Experiencing Blake's work, particularly the books he created using the illuminated printing method, is transformative for many. In *Songs of Innocence*, the painter and poet combine to show us childhood. Reading his poetry and immersing ourselves in his designs can, as Blake himself said, cleanse 'the doors of perception', reminding children in the digital age that childhood is a time of exuberance and of social and ecological connection, and returning adults to a time and space they may have thought lost. With his unique combination of the verbal and visual, Blake prompts our imaginations to revisit notions of play, harmony, and spontaneity, where the defining traits of the world are compassion, empathy, and love.

Mark Crosby

NOTE

Blake's spelling is not always consistent with modern standards and his punctuation can, at times, be challenging to decipher. The transcriptions that follow preserve what can be read in this version of *Songs of Innocence*.

SONGS
OF
Innocence

The Author & Printer W. Blake

Introduction

Piping down the valleys wild
Piping songs of pleasant glee
On a cloud I saw a child.
And he laughing said to me.

Pipe a song about a Lamb:
So I piped with merry chear,
Piper pipe that song again—
So I piped, he wept to hear.

Drop thy pipe thy happy pipe
Sing thy songs of happy chear,
So I sung the same again
While he wept with joy to hear

Piper sit thee down and write
In a book that all may read—
So he vanish'd from my sight.
And I pluck'd a hollow reed.

And I made a rural pen,
And I stain'd the water clear,
And I wrote my happy songs,
Every child may joy to hear

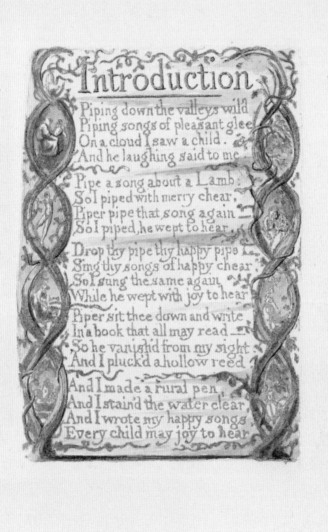

Introduction

Piping down the valleys wild
Piping songs of pleasant glee
On a cloud I saw a child.
And he laughing said to me.

Pipe a song about a Lamb:
So I piped with merry chear,
Piper pipe that song again—
So I piped, he wept to hear.

Drop thy pipe thy happy pipe
Sing thy songs of happy chear,
So I sung the same again
While he wept with joy to hear

Piper sit thee down and write
In a book that all may read—
So he vanish'd from my sight
And I pluck'd a hollow reed.

And I made a rural pen,
And I stain'd the water clear,
And I wrote my happy songs
Every child may joy to hear

The Shepherd.

How sweet is the Shepherds sweet lot.
From the morn to the evening he strays;
He shall follow his sheep all the day.
And his tongue shall be filled with praise.

For he hears the lambs innocent call.
And he hears the ewes tender reply.
He is watchful while they are in peace.
For they know when their Shepherd is nigh.

The Shepherd.

How sweet is the Shepherds sweet lot!
From the morn to the evening he strays;
He shall follow his sheep all the day,
And his tongue shall be filled with praise.

For he hears the lambs innocent call,
And he hears the ewes tender reply,
He is watchful while they are in peace,
For they know when their Shepherd is nigh.

Infant Joy

I have no name
I am but two days old.—
What shall I call thee?
I happy am
Joy is my name,—
Sweet joy befall thee!

Pretty joy!
Sweet joy but two days old,
Sweet joy I call thee;
Thou dost smile.
I sing the while
Sweet joy befall thee.

Infant Joy

I have no name
I am but two days old —
What shall I call thee?
I happy am
Joy is my name —
Sweet joy befall thee!

Pretty joy!
Sweet joy but two days old,
Sweet joy I call thee;
Thou dost smile.
I sing the while
Sweet joy befall thee.

Nurse's Song

When the voices of children are heard on the green
And laughing is heard on the hill,
My heart is at rest within my breast
And every thing else is still

Then come home my children the sun is gone down
And the dews of night arise
Come come leave off play, and let us away
Till the morning appears in the skies

No no let us play, for it is yet day
And we cannot go to sleep
Besides in the sky the little birds fly
And the hills are all coverd with sheep

Well well go & play till the light fades away
And then go home to bed
The little ones leaped & shouted & laugh'd
And all the hills ecchoed

Nurses Song

When the voices of children are heard on the green
And laughing is heard on the hill,
My heart is at rest within my breast
And every thing else is still

Then come home my children the sun is gone down
And the dews of night arise
Come come leave off play, and let us away
Till the morning appears in the skies

No no let us play, for it is yet day
And we cannot go to sleep
Besides in the sky the little birds fly
And the hills are all coverd with sheep

Well well go & play till the light fades away
And then go home to bed
The little ones leaped & shouted & laugh'd
And all the hills eccho'd

HOLY THURSDAY

Twas on a Holy Thursday their innocent faces clean
The children walking two & two in red & blue & green
                                                    (snow
Grey headed beadles walkd before with wands as white as
Till into the high dome of Pauls they like Thames waters flow

O what a multitude they seemd these flowers of London town
Seated in companies they sit, with radiance all their own
The hum of multitudes was there but multitudes of lambs
Thousands of little boys & girls raising their innocent hands

Now like a mighty wind they raise to heaven the voice of song
Or like harmonious thunderings the seats of heaven among
Beneath them sit the aged men wise guardians of the poor
Then cherish pity, lest you drive an angel from your door

HOLY THURSDAY

Twas on a Holy Thursday their innocent faces clean
The children walking two & two in red & blue & green
Grey headed beadles walked before with wands as white as snow
Till into the high dome of Pauls they like Thames waters flow

O what a multitude they seemd these flowers of London town
Seated in companies they sit with radiance all their own
The hum of multitudes was there but multitudes of lambs
Thousands of little boys & girls raising their innocent hands

Now like a mighty wind they raise to heaven the voice of song
Or like harmonious thunderings the seats of heaven among
Beneath them sit the aged men wise guardians of the poor
Then cherish pity. lest you drive an angel from your door

On Anothers Sorrow

Can I see anothers woe.
And not be in sorrow too.
Can I see anothers grief.
And not seek for kind relief.

Can I see a falling tear.
And not feel my sorrows share,
Can a father see his child.
Weep, nor be with sorrow fill'd.

Can a mother sit and hear.
An infant groan an infant fear—
No no never can it be.
Never never can it be.

And can he who smiles on all
Hear the wren with sorrows small.
Hear the small birds grief & care
Hear the woes that infants bear—

And not sit beside the nest
Pouring pity in their breast.
And not sit the cradle near
Weeping tear on infants tear.

And not sit both night & day.
Wiping all our tears away.
O! no never can it be.
Never never can it be.

He doth give his joy to all.
He becomes an infant small.
He becomes a man of woe
He doth feel the sorrow too.

Think not. thou canst sigh a sigh,
And thy maker is not by.
Think not. thou canst weep a tear,
And thy maker is not near.

O! he gives to us his joy.
That our grief he may destroy
Till our grief is fled & gone
He doth sit by us and moan

On Anothers Sorrow

Can I see anothers woe,
And not be in sorrow too.
Can I see anothers grief
And not seek for kind relief.

Can I see a falling tear,
And not feel my sorrows share,
Can a father see his child
Weep, nor be with sorrow filld.

Can a mother sit and hear,
An infant groan an infant fear—
No no never can it be,
Never never can it be.

And can he who smiles on all
Hear the wren with sorrows small
Hear the small birds grief & care
Hear the woes that infants bear—

And not sit beside the nest
Pouring pity in their breast,
And not sit the cradle near
Weeping tear on infants tear.

And not sit both night & day
Wiping all our tears away.
O! no never can it be.
Never never can it be.

He doth give his joy to all,
He becomes an infant small.
He becomes a man of woe
He doth feel the sorrow too.

Think not thou canst sigh a sigh,
And thy maker is not by.
Think not thou canst weep a tear
And thy maker is not near.

O! he gives to us his joy.
That our grief he may destroy
Till our grief is fled & gone
He doth sit by us and moan

Spring

Sound the Flute!
Now its mute.
Birds delight
Day and Night.
Nightingale
In the dale
Lark in Sky
Merrily   (Year
Merrily Merrily to Welcome in the

Little Boy
Full of joy.

                              Little

Spring

Sound the Flute!
Now it's mute.
Birds delight
Day and Night.
Nightingale
In the dale
Lark in Sky
Merrily   Year
Merrily Merrily to welcome in the

Little Boy
Full of joy.

                                           Little

Little Girl
Sweet and small.
Cock does crow
So do you.
Merry voice
Infant noise
Merrily Merrily to welcome in the Year

Little Lamb
Here I am,
Come and lick
My white neck.
Let me pull
Your soft Wool.
Let me kiss
Your soft face.   Year
Merrily Merrily we welcome in the

Little Girl
Sweet and small.
Cock does crow
So do you.
Merry voice
Infant noise
Merrily Merrily to welcome in the Year

Little Lamb
Here I am
Come and lick
My white neck.
Let me pull
Your soft Wool
Let me kiss
Your soft face ....   Year
Merrily Merrily we welcome in the

The School Boy

I love to rise in a summer morn.
When the birds sing on every tree;
The distant huntsman winds his horn.
And the sky-lark sings with me.
O! what sweet company.

But to go to school in a summer morn,
O! it drives all joy away;
Under a cruel eye outworn.
The little ones spend the day.
In sighing and dismay.

Ah! then at times I drooping sit.
And spend many an anxious hour.
Nor in my book can I take delight,
Nor sit in learnings bower.
Worn thro' with the dreary shower.

How can the bird that is born for joy,
Sit in a cage and sing.
How can a child when fears annoy.
But droop his tender wing.
And forget his youthful spring.

O! father & mother, if buds are nip'd,
And blossoms blown away.
And if the tender plants are strip'd
Of their joy in the springing day,
By sorrow and cares dismay.

How shall the summer arise in joy.
Or the summer fruits appear.   (troy
Or how shall we gather what griefs des
Or bless the mellowing year.
When the blasts of winter appear.

The School Boy

I love to rise in a summer morn,
When the birds sing on every tree;
The distant huntsman winds his horn,
And the sky-lark sings with me.
O! what sweet company.

But to go to school in a summer morn,
O! it drives all joy away;
Under a cruel eye outworn,
The little ones spend the day,
In sighing and dismay.

Ah! then at times I drooping sit,
And spend many an anxious hour,
Nor in my book can I take delight,
Nor sit in learnings bower,
Worn thro' with the dreary shower.

How can the bird that is born for joy,
Sit in a cage and sing.
How can a child when fears annoy,
But droop his tender wing,
And forget his youthful spring.

O! father & mother, if buds are nip'd,
And blossoms blown away,
And if the tender plants are strip'd
Of their joy in the springing day,
By sorrow and cares dismay.

How shall the summer arise in joy,
Or the summer fruits appear.
Or how shall we gather what griefs destroy
Or bless the mellowing year,
When the blasts of winter appear.

Laughing Song

When the green woods laugh. with the voice of joy
And the dimpling stream runs laughing by,
When the air does laugh with our merry wit,
And the green hill laughs with the noise of it.

When the meadows laugh with lively green
And the grasshopper laughs in the merry scene,
When Mary and Susan and Emily,
With their sweet round mouths sing Ha, Ha, He.

When the painted birds laugh in the shade
Where our table with cherries and nuts is spread
Come live & be merry and join with me,
To sing the sweet chorus of Ha, Ha, He.

Laughing Song

When the green woods laugh with the voice of joy
And the dimpling stream runs laughing by,
When the air does laugh with our merry wit,
And the green hill laughs with the noise of it.

When the meadows laugh with lively green
And the grasshopper laughs in the merry scene,
When Mary and Susan and Emily,
With their sweet round mouths sing Ha, Ha, He.

When the painted birds laugh in the shade
Where our table with cherries and nuts is spread
Come live & be merry and join with me,
To sing the sweet chorus of Ha, Ha, He.

The Little Black Boy

My mother bore me in the southern wild,
And I am black, but O! my soul is white
White as an angel is the English child:
But I am black as if bereav'd of light.

My mother taught me underneath a tree
And sitting down before the heat of day.
She took me on her lap and kissed me.
And pointing to the east began to say.

Look on the rising sun! there God does live
And gives his light and gives his heat away.
And flowers and trees and beasts and men recieve
Comfort in morning joy in the noon day.

And we are put on earth a little space.
That we may learn to bear the beams of love.
And these black bodies and this sun-burnt face
Is but a cloud, and like a shady grove.

For

The Little Black Boy

My mother bore me in the southern wild,
And I am black, but O! my soul is white;
White as an angel is the English child:
But I am black as if bereav'd of light.

My mother taught me underneath a tree,
And sitting down before the heat of day,
She took me on her lap and kissed me,
And pointing to the east began to say.

Look on the rising sun: there God does live
And gives his light, and gives his heat away,
And flowers and trees and beasts and men receive
Comfort in morning joy in the noon day.

And we are put on earth a little space,
That we may learn to bear the beams of love,
And these black bodies and this sun-burnt face
Is but a cloud, and like a shady grove.

For

For when our souls have learn'd the heat to bear
The cloud will vanish we shall hear his voice
Saying: come out from the grove my love & care,
And round my golden tent like lambs rejoice.

Thus did my mother say and kissed me.
And thus I say to little English boy.
When I from black and he from white cloud free.
And round the tent of God like lambs we joy:

Ill shade him from the heat till he can bear,
To lean in joy upon our fathers knee.
And then I'll stand and stroke his silver hair,
And be like him and he will then love me.

For when our souls have learn'd the heat to bear
The cloud will vanish we shall hear his voice.
Saying: come out from the grove my love & care
And round my golden tent like lambs rejoice.

Thus did my mother say and kissed me,
And thus I say to little English boy.
When I from black and he from white cloud free
And round the tent of God like lambs we joy:

I'll shade him from the heat till he can bear,
To lean in joy upon our fathers knee
And then I'll stand and stroke his silver hair
And be like him and he will then love me.

The Voice of the Ancient Bard.

Youth of delight come hither,
And see the opening morn,
Image of truth new-born
Doubt is fled & clouds of reason.
Dark disputes & artful teazing.
Folly is an endless maze.
Tangled roots perplex her ways.
How many have fallen there!
They stumble all night over bones of the dead;
And feel they know not what but care;
And wish to lead others when they should be led.

The Voice of the Ancient Bard.

Youth of delight come hither
And see the opening morn,
Image of truth new born.
Doubt is fled & clouds of reason.
Dark disputes & artful teazing.
Folly is an endless maze,
Tangled roots perplex her ways,
How many have fallen there!
They stumble all night over bones of the dead;
And feel they know not what but care;
And wish to lead others when they should be led.

The Ecchoing Green

The Sun does arise,
And make happy the skies
The merry bells ring
To welcome the Spring.
The sky-lark and thrush.
The birds of the bush,
Sing louder around,
To the bells chearful sound.
While our sports shall be seen
On the Ecchoing Green.

Old John with white hair
Does laugh away care,
Sitting under the oak,
Among the old folk,

They

The Ecchoing Green

The Sun does arise,
And make happy the skies.
The merry bells ring
To welcome the Spring.
The sky-lark and thrush,
The birds of the bush,
Sing louder around,
To the bells cheerful sound.
While our sports shall be seen
On the Ecchoing Green.

Old John with white hair
Does laugh away care,
Sitting under the oak,
Among the old folk,

They laugh at our play.
And soon they all say.
Such such were the joys.
When we all girls & boys.
In our youth-time were seen,
On the Ecchoing Green.

Till the little ones weary
No more can be merry
The sun does descend.
And our sports have an end:
Round the laps of their mothers.
Many sisters and brothers.
Like birds in their nest,
Are ready for rest:
And sport no more seen,
On the darkening Green.

They laugh at our play,
And soon they all say,
Such such were the joys,
When we all girls & boys,
In our youth time were seen,
On the Ecchoing Green.

Till the little ones weary
No more can be merry
The sun does descend,
And our sports have an end:
Round the laps of their mothers,
Many sisters and brothers
Like birds in their nest,
Are ready for rest:
And sport no more seen,
On the darkening Green.

A CRADLE SONG

Sweet dreams form a shade.
O'er my lovely infants head.
Sweet dreams of pleasant streams.
By happy silent moony beams

Sweet sleep with soft down.
Weave thy brows an infant crown.
Sweet sleep Angel mild,
Hover o'er my happy child.

Sweet smiles in the night.
Hover over my delight.
Sweet smiles Mothers smiles
All the livelong night beguiles.

Sweet moans. dovelike sighs.
Chase not slumber from thy eyes.
Sweet moans. sweeter smiles.
All the dovelike moans beguiles.

Sleep sleep happy child.
All creation slept and smil'd.
Sleep sleep, happy sleep.
While o'er thee thy mother weep

Sweet babe in thy face.
Holy image I can trace.
Sweet babe once like thee.
Thy maker lay and wept for me

Wept

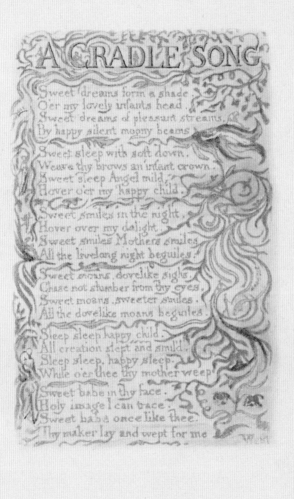

A CRADLE SONG

Sweet dreams form a shade,
O'er my lovely infants head.
Sweet dreams of pleasant streams,
By happy silent moony beams

Sweet sleep with soft down.
Weave thy brows an infant crown.
Sweet sleep Angel mild,
Hover o'er my happy child.

Sweet smiles in the night,
Hover over my delight,
Sweet smiles Mothers smiles,
All the livelong night beguiles.

Sweet moans, dovelike sighs,
Chase not slumber from thy eyes,
Sweet moans, sweeter smiles,
All the dovelike moans beguiles.

Sleep sleep happy child,
All creation slept and smild.
Sleep sleep, happy sleep,
While o'er thee thy mother weep

Sweet babe in thy face,
Holy image I can trace.
Sweet babe once like thee,
Thy maker lay and wept for me

Wept for me for thee for all.
When he was an infant small.
Thou his image ever see.
Heavenly face that smiles on thee.

Smiles on thee on me on all.
Who became an infant small.
Infant smiles are his own smiles.
Heaven & earth to peace beguiles.

Wept for me for thee for all.
When he was an infant small.
Thou his image ever see.
Heavenly face that smiles on thee

Smiles on thee on me on all
Who became an infant small.
Infant smiles are his own smiles.
Heaven & earth to peace beguiles

The Little Boy lost

Father, father, where are you going
O do not walk so fast.
Speak father. speak to your little boy
Or else I shall be lost.

The night was dark no father was there
The child was wet with dew.
The mire was deep, & the child did weep
And away the vapour flew

The Little Boy lost

Father, father where are you going
O do not walk so fast.
Speak father, speak to your little boy
Or else I shall be lost.

The night was dark no father was there
The child was wet with dew.
The mire was deep, & the child did weep
And away the vapour flew

The Little Boy found

The little boy lost in the lonely fen.
Led by the wand'ring light,
Began to cry, but God ever nigh.
Appeard like his father in white.

He kissed the child & by the hand led
And to his mother brought.
Who in sorrow pale, thro' the lonely dale
Her little boy weeping sought.

The Little Boy found

The little boy lost in the lonely fen,
Led by the wandring light,
Began to cry, but God ever nigh,
Appeard like his father in white.

He kissed the child & by the hand led
And to his mother brought,
Who in sorrow pale, thro' the lonely dale
Her little boy weeping sought.

The Lamb

Little Lamb who made thee
  Dost thou know who made thee
Gave thee life & bid thee feed.
By the stream & o'er the mead;
Gave thee clothing of delight,
Softest clothing wooly bright;
Gave thee such a tender voice.
Making all the vales rejoice:
  Little Lamb who made thee
  Dost thou know who made thee

  Little Lamb Ill tell thee,
  Little Lamb Ill tell thee:
He is called by thy name,
For he calls himself a Lamb:
He is meek & he is mild,
He became a little child:
I a child & thou a lamb.
We are called by his name.
  Little Lamb God bless thee.
  Little Lamb God bless thee.

The Lamb

Little Lamb who made thee
Dost thou know who made thee
Gave thee life & bid thee feed.
By the stream & o'er the mead;
Gave thee clothing of delight,
Softest clothing wooly bright;
Gave thee such a tender voice,
Making all the vales rejoice:
Little Lamb who made thee
Dost thou know who made thee

Little Lamb I'll tell thee,
Little Lamb I'll tell thee;
He is called by thy name,
For he calls himself a Lamb:
He is meek & he is mild;
He became a little child:
I a child & thou a lamb.
We are called by his name.
Little Lamb God bless thee.
Little Lamb God bless thee.

The Blossom.

Merry Merry Sparrow
Under leaves so green
A happy Blossom
Sees you swift as arrow
Seek your cradle narrow
Near my Bosom.

Pretty Pretty Robin
Under leaves so green
A happy Blossom
Hears you sobbing sobbing
Pretty Pretty Robin
Near my Bosom.

The Blossom.

Merry Merry Sparrow
Under leaves so green
A happy Blossom
Sees you swift as arrow
Seek your cradle narrow
Near my Bosom.

Pretty Pretty Robin
Under leaves so green
A happy Blossom
Hears you sobbing sobbing
Pretty Pretty Robin
Near my Bosom.

The Divine Image.

To Mercy Pity Peace and Love.
All pray in their distress:
And to these virtues of delight
Return their thankfulness.

For Mercy Pity Peace and Love,
Is God our father dear:
And Mercy Pity Peace and Love.
Is Man his child and care.

For Mercy has a human heart
Pity, a human face:
And Love, the human form divine.
And Peace, the human dress.

Then every man of every clime,
That prays in his distress,
Prays to the human form divine
Love Mercy Pity Peace.

And all must love the human form,
In heathen, turk or jew
Where Mercy, Love & Pity dwell
There God is dwelling too

The Divine Image.

To Mercy Pity Peace and Love,
All pray in their distress;
And to these virtues of delight
Return their thankfulness.

For Mercy Pity Peace and Love,
Is God our father dear;
And Mercy Pity Peace and Love,
Is Man his child and care.

For Mercy has a human heart
Pity, a human face:
And Love, the human form divine,
And Peace, the human dress.

Then every man of every clime,
That prays in his distress,
Prays to the human form divine
Love Mercy Pity Peace.

And all must love the human form,
In heathen turk or jew
Where Mercy, Love & Pity dwell,
There God is dwelling too.

The Chimney Sweeper

When my mother died I was very young.
And my father sold me while yet
  my tongue,
Could scarcely cry weep weep
  weep weep.
So your chimneys I sweep & in soot
  I sleep.

Theres little Tom Dacre. who cried when
  his head
(That curl'd like a lambs back, was
  shav'd, so I said:
Hush Tom never mind it, for when your
  head's bare.
You know that the soot cannot spoil your
  white hair.

And so he was quiet, & that very night.
As Tom was a sleeping he had such
  a sight,
That thousands of sweepers Dick, Joe,
  Ned & Jack
Were all of them lock'd up in coffins
  of black.

And by came an Angel who had a
  bright key
And he open'd the coffins & set them all
  free.

Then down a green plain leaping
  laughing they run
And wash in a river and shine in the Sun.

Then naked & white, all their bags
  left behind.
They rise upon clouds, and sport in
  the wind.
And the Angel told Tom if he'd be a
  good boy.
He'd have God for his father & never
  want joy.

And so Tom awoke and we rose in
  the dark
And got with our bags & our brushes
  to work.
Tho' the morning was cold, Tom was
  happy & warm.
So if all do their duty, they need not
  fear harm.

The Chimney Sweeper

When my mother died I was very young,
And my father sold me while yet my tongue,
Could scarcely cry weep weep weep weep.
So your chimneys I sweep & in soot I sleep.

Theres little Tom Dacre, who cried when his head
That curld like a lambs back, was shav'd, so I said.
Hush Tom never mind it, for when your heads bare,
You know that the soot cannot spoil your white hair.

And so he was quiet, & that very night,
As Tom was a sleeping he had such a sight,
That thousands of sweepers Dick, Joe, Ned & Jack
Were all of them lock'd up in coffins of black,

And by came an Angel who had a bright key,
And he opend the coffins & set them all free.
Then down a green plain leaping laughing they run
And wash in a river and shine in the Sun.

Then naked & white, all their bags left behind,
They rise upon clouds, and sport in the wind.
And the Angel told Tom if he'd be a good boy,
He'd have God for his father & never want joy.

And so Tom awoke and we rose in the dark
And got with our bags & our brushes to work.
Tho' the morning was cold, Tom was happy & warm,
So if all do their duty, they need not fear harm.

Night

The sun descending in the west.
The evening star does shine.
The birds are silent in their nest.
And I must seek for mine,
The moon like a flower.
In heavens high bower:
With silent delight.
Sits and smiles on the night.

Farewell green fields and happy groves,
Where flocks have took delight;
Where lambs have nibbled, silent moves
The feet of angels bright;
Unseen they pour blessing.
And joy without ceasing.
On each bud and blossom.
And each sleeping bosom.

They look in every thoughtless nest.
Where birds are coverd warm;
They visit caves of every beast
To keep them all from harm;
If they see any weeping.
That should have been sleeping
They pour sleep on their head
And sit down by their bed.

When

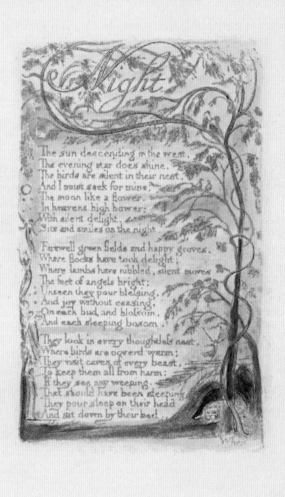

Night

The sun descending in the west,
The evening star does shine.
The birds are silent in their nest,
And I must seek for mine,
The moon like a flower,
In heavens high bower;
With silent delight,
Sits and smiles on the night.

Farewell green fields and happy groves,
Where flocks have took delight;
Where lambs have nibbled, silent moves
The feet of angels bright;
Unseen they pour blessing,
And joy without ceasing,
On each bud and blossom,
And each sleeping bosom.

They look in every thoughtless nest,
Where birds are cover'd warm;
They visit caves of every beast,
To keep them all from harm:
If they see any weeping,
That should have been sleeping,
They pour sleep on their head
And sit down by their bed.

When wolves and tygers howl for prey
They pitying stand and weep;
Seeking to drive their thirst away.
And keep them from the sheep.
But if they rush dreadful;
The angels most heedful,
Recieve each mild spirit.
New worlds to inherit.

And there the lions ruddy eyes.
Shall flow with tears of gold:
And pitying the tender cries.
And walking round the fold:
Saying: wrath by his meekness
And by his health. sickness.
Is driven away.
From our immortal day.

And now beside thee bleating lamb.
I can lie down and sleep;
Or think on him who bore thy name.
Grase after thee and weep.
For wash'd in lifes river.
My bright mane for ever.
Shall shine like the gold.
As I guard o'er the fold.

When wolves and tygers howl for prey
They pitying stand and weep;
Seeking to drive their thirst away,
And keep them from the sheep
But if they rush dreadful;
The angels most heedful,
Recieve each mild spirit,
New worlds to inherit.

And there the lions ruddy eyes,
Shall flow with tears of gold:
And pitying the tender cries,
And walking round the fold:
Saying: wrath by his meekness
And by his health, sickness,
Is driven away.
From our immortal day.

And now beside thee bleating lamb,
I can lie down and sleep;
Or think on him who bore thy name
Graze after thee and weep.
For wash'd in lifes river,
My bright mane for ever,
Shall shine like the gold,
As I guard o'er the fold.